ARCHITECTURE
FOR A
THIRD AMERICAN REPUBLIC

A Political Science Perspective
Upon the Realistic Options for
Some Form of Continuance of American Ideals
In a Possible Post-American World

By
Robert B. Cronkhite

Dedication
To my brother, David Michael Cronkhite,
who is so long missed and
who was a pugilist and a risk taker literally
to the ends of God's earth.

Edited by Susan Reyes Morrison

Table of Contents

A History Untangled

It has become sadly obvious that resulting consequences of the nineteenth century's policies of Reconstruction following the assassination of President Abraham Lincoln have failed in "forming a more perfect union", even of *union* itself. A government, that does not follow its foundations of ethics and human rights, in consideration for the common good and even education for preparation to compete in a more educated and complex world, is a fallacy; even a ***tyranny***.

After over 140 years of a baseless government that has been less and less anchored upon the Articles of Confederation, the Constitution and even with supposed Amendments since the 'War Between the States' or the Civil War, has left a nation adrift and lost.

Consider a day to come when finally a people takes back its own government, to follow and enforce its original Articles of Confederation and its Constitution; away from those who have, since the Johnson and Grant administrations sold it by subterfuge unto the greedy institutions of then and now; only intending promise and growth, while as a cloud that promises rain delivers so little, to none.

Proposal of Secession

It is upon the course of history that when a People, being firmly oppressed by an unconstitutional, federal system, may seek by any peaceful means available their state's right to secede from such a union.

That a People thus shall purpose a better, more legal republic based on the Articles of Confederation and the original, un-amended Constitution; to pursue upon themselves purpose of history not entangled upon false and illegal precepts of which this current government has continued since Reconstruction and the illegal end of the *First American Republic of 1776*; having been replaced by federalist and corrupt elements to the detriment of the original concepts and organization of the Articles of Confederation and the Constitution; replacing such from an illegal amalgamation of states by force usurping the rights of the states and the people of original intent.

Thusly, on the 4th of July, 2014 (2015 or 2016) this illegal *Second Republic* and its capital Washington, D.C. is null and void of all political power, replaced by Oklahoma City, OK; and upon such time of 1200 noon EDT that Washington, D.C. is surrounded for preparation of trial of treason, all personnel and facilities, by the legal *Third American Republic* military forces.

"Welcome to the *Third American Republic,* and may God's will be done! "   I do offer this as the growing cry for a judicious return of the 'original republic' in this declaration.

Now with Precedents,
We are Permitted to Establish the *Third Republic*

As per the United Nations and the public justification, based upon declaration such as for a Palestinian State already underway, we too without dissent from any quarter do similarly resolve. Now with such unremitting precedents, we are permitted to establish the ***Third American Republic***. In the present day practice of only by declaring for a new state, this by its accepted practice in the world, also establishes the vitality of a 'Christian Zionist State'. As per the original Articles of Confederation and the Constitution with only the original ten Amendments to again start from, this as a valid state as any other by such same means being proposed, has also to be honored. If one is not for any reason to be honored, then the other is not. For upon the basis of logic and unprejudiced, true, mature, objective thought, then a 'Christian Zionist State' is offered for the voluntarily seceded states to re-establish their rightful confederation, again under the lawful foundation of the Articles of Confederation and the Constitution.

Consequences of Returning to Original Intent

Only property taxes were allowed in the original intentions. There would be no income taxes, for what the laborer earned, would rightfully be one's own and no other's. Direct representation is practical with the acceptance by even the present commercial, educational and governmental parts of society, so there is no logical need for career representatives. In the results of such representation based on past history, only direct representation would allow the people to finally govern themselves. Any lobbying would have to provide influence to all and thus liquidate those lobbyists' personally favored targets quite expensively. Only the People would be the ones to raise, lower or end a 'servant of the people's' salary. No longer needing representatives, the People themselves would be the public servants, finally serving the public.

All government officials would no longer find any immunity from the law, but would suffer the punishments as according to the 'Court of the People'. A representative of the People would act as an ambassador for the *Third Republic*, replacing the present tyranny of presidents unwilling to execute the laws of the land.

Another Continental Congress is of need: as to again give voice and consideration based on logic, ethics and common sense of all citizens and for the common good and the re-establishment of law and decency in the land. The criminal acts of thievery under the guise of 'public domain' would return all lands to the people, including remaining descendants.

Each citizen is to be awarded $100,000 tax free from the treasury to re-establish a free economy, spur growth and a healthy prosperity. Wholesome industry of labor, factory, research, development, education, and academics would be returned to the function of a healthy and ethical society. Rather than unprofitable wars of aggression, only those necessary for the defense and the pursuit of advancing a desirable society of life, liberty and the pursuit of happiness to all would be engaged

This *Third Republic* would be a beacon, rather than in its present deterioration, a warning to the rest of the world. It would be a republic not a 'democracy' resulting in greed-based anarchy for business and common, but accountable to the people. Finally the *People*, the individual citizens as the prime governing body "We the People", would have its proper worth and respect.

History Has Spoken,
Only a Decisive Change Remains

There are many trying to adjure others to their own personal, self-centered philosophies against any and all Judeo-Christian based belief systems. These same attempt to 'prove' the lack of authentication for the Bible, Jesus Christ as The Son of God and the basis of western civilization's ethics, albeit imperfect; yet continually fail to support their own supposedly 'indisputable proofs' for their lack of belief in faith systems. As history speaks, it has at least shown true objectivity in human reasoning: from 'pure' science, to 'pure' history, to 'pure' theology, to 'pure' atheism- all repeatedly failed to win converts of the thinking variety to either of their sides. No one is really 'purely' objective enough to reason and leave potential converts without any of the haunting doubts that hypocrites of the 'scientifically objective fact' cannot authenticate themselves.

Often the claimed debates of 'reason' are really just the continual academic, adversarial, monotonous banter between 'objective' antagonists, who in the final analysis were both incapable of proving any immutable authentications that can withstand any true repeatable, scientific evidence.

Thus, all is one religion versus another religion, belief system versus belief system, without the needed decisive changes.

As Daniel Webster has defined, "all religions are also belief systems"; thusly even an agnostic's or an atheist's belief system can only reflect their 'faith', just as any Judeo-Christian can theirs, observable by their fruits and the repeatable, verifiable, scientific evidence that limited humanity can only vaguely perceive. All else is 'faith' beyond the limits of any human reason.

To an observing, neutral, third party it would seem to be the continuation of the supposedly 'objective', 'unbiased', countering presentations; ridiculous attempts of each side trying to prove what they cannot, and to convince by limited human observations and measurements, what is really an impossible conclusion. Both are avoiding what is obvious to any non-participating third party of how ignorant both sides really are. God, evolution, climate change and politics have been, are and always will be continually debated. It is as if the two 'academics' are only showing that after enough 'education', humans would rather fight than cooperate; that academics is as reflective of our war-like nature symbolically as the war profiteers and their empire builders are in practice.

This may be the answer to the trend of historical evidence as to why humanity is alone unto itself and thus our achievements and claims repeatedly cannot really do anything to improve our human condition. What is being repeatedly proven by all academic adversaries is only that humanistic aspirations are delusional. The humanists challenge, but do not want to be challenged. They claim to be tolerant, but only show their intolerance even unto mental, emotional and physical cruelty. In trying to disprove the Bible, they are actually proving its principles of the real potential of Godless humanity and its tyrannical fruit. They try to control and sway; but if one really thinks of their potential converts, really sees and hears, why would one desire their tragedy of depreciation of human fruition? Their repeated, stubborn, unauthenticated foundations show only a neurotic selfish ignorance. They have not, are not and will not prove their religion. They, after the initial mask of their facade falls away, become more frustrated, warlike and simply reflect their hypocrisy.

Revolution, of and for only revolution, is the anarchists' world that brings first a temporary satisfaction and then destroys itself. Even within the imperfect, remaining traces of historical records, all capitalist, socialist and communist systems remove any remaining revolutionaries who just continue to be disruptive anarchists. It is from the spoiling by some unlimited prosperity of economics and time that seems to be the seedbed for such unjust seeking 'justice'. Actual constructive change, rather than long wasted argumentation is now required. A cake cannot without end stay in an oven or it will never be partaken of; a baby one day has to leave the cradle, learn to walk, then run; so people eventually need to realize their promised ideals.

"We the People"

In this day and age of the personal computer, it is imperative to the real test of a People to actually demonstrate the governing of themselves. If we all take claim to the proposal of a free and active personal republic, then we shall not shirk from its finally being a realization. No more the need of representatives bought, sold and lobbied by the secret sabotage of the hidden selfish interests. Now, if one is to be lobbied, then all are lobbied; thus it will become such an expensive endeavor upon those practicing that influence against the common good.

To have a head of state, as per a president, is fine. But all such ambassadors of the citizenry are no longer beyond the reach of law and self-sufficient economic support. They would be limited to a short term and none for a career, so as to avoid the historically observed graft and corruptive practices of traitors. 'Economic' treason, as well as military and all forms of such destruction of the 'common good', would be of equal consequence. What was good for the lowest scoundrel on the lowest rung of the social ladder is as good for the top echelon of any elite to surface; thusly, each and every citizen is qualified, as any other to serve at any level of government. With also the attendant advisors as needed for each, yet all in full range of the consequences of the law, or full rewards of achievements, upon the woe or benefit of the common good.

Redistricting under the newly-established *Third American Republic* could redraw county and state boundaries in response to the prior damages to the intentions of the *First and Second Republics*, known as the 'United States of America'. This *Third American Republic* being understood as the proper confederation of the states, with this 'confederation' being its unity and not its oppression of a united tyranny, thus far historically perpetuated. This prior 'union', operated by subtle and overt force, has not worked as was philosophized since the founding of each republic.

The Revolution of the 18th century, followed by the civil warfare of 1812 and then the 'War Between the States' from 1861 to 1864, have not been able to solve the repeated frustrations that led to these conflicts of selfish individual and corporate interests versus the proposed common good of the people. A result of the actual course in history of blatant and subtle disregard for such contracts between the governing and the governed, are these civil warfares. To promise, as it is written, a rain cloud and yet deliver none, is but the succinct cause of the repeated failure for the full potential of the people really governing themselves; as if the governing is non-verbally stating that such promised hope is really too dangerous for their self-interests of tyranny because of gilded false hopes.

A true patriotism of the citizens, individual and corporate, would better be for the 'common good'. *We the People* can move finally from theory to practice; and more, its realization of its full potential would so intelligently reset the erasure of our nation. The practiced graft and corruption of economic, social and political treasons recorded in its actual history has been the ulcer of conflict; as is the consequential usurping from the people their rightful inheritance of the proper republic so long promised. Influence has so subtle an effect; good, as well as bad is a progressive entity in the arts of persuasion, whether a person, corporation or the government they allow themselves to be under.

Thinking as humanly possible, as we are limited in the ideal of motives, advertising and propaganda are such kindred things. One self-promoting ideology trying to convince another that it is somehow inadequate in comparison .... if the self-promoting idea is assertive and stubborn enough, then when the other refuses long enough, the self-promoting ideal just bullies by way of intellect, emotion and then eventually physically to get its tyrannical desperate way … will become an hypocrisy of its own values and eventually destroy its own self. "Power corrupts, and absolute power corrupts absolutely", especially when hiding behind the mask of supposed 'enlightenment and benevolence'.

Pity No Difference Between Nation or Gang

Sadly, for the governed there is no difference from a tyrannical leadership, whether individual, corporate, national or religious; it is belligerent despite its particular masks of 'enlightenment and benevolence' and needs to overcome any other by continually persuading for just its own selfish welfare. Such is the pitiful suffering of the governed; as prey, to be seeing and hearing of no difference from a nation or a gang; a tyrant, as always, is still a *tyrant*.

But for a constructive change we need to have an architecture upon which to build. "We the People", we who are the citizens, need to directly run the course of *our* government. It has been promoted since this nation's early beginnings, why not actually put it to ground truth? With the personal computer and a basically intelligent populous we can really have a nation, not a polished gang, in the purpose of representing 'We', the constituency.

As so often in human history, the lack of 'definition-agreement' arouses conflict from the political, social, economic, religious and even academic arenas.

The faith versus the rationalist is so many times revealed amongst the debating that goes on and on with neither side able to convince the other to satisfaction. Rather, the ingrained human traits of selfish manipulation, when frustrated, verbal to even physical combat repeatedly results.

Again under Daniel Webster's definition that "religion is a system of ideas": all these 'religions' are really only vying for their own advantage, seeming to never complete their arguments to help humankind reach the next step in our willful progression. God is forgotten or just in the way, even for so many of the 'religious'. Jesus did not teach of religion, He taught of relationship. There is such a grand difference that so many of the 'enlightened' stumble backwards, with the next time only to repeat their ever-widening circle of the *raisons de etre* which has become the still-spinning broken record.

In order to really accomplish anything, the overly, isolated, ivory-towered tyrants of selfish interests have to be maturely ignored. Those who really think and are trying to understand and make a better world, just have to make their view of a better world and with God, so much the better.

In my living longer, my overly obsessive, rationalistic effort is as much a sickness, as too little …. as any unbalanced zealousness to this author; after decades of debates about faith in God, evolution, rationalist tyrannies and life on other planets, I find by my patiently observing and measuring the repeated evidence, in longer and longer durations of time, the 'wondered-about' is more and more proven or disproven. As a scientist, to me God is more real; *Inherent Differentiation* seems the real biological mechanism of diverted lives' topological geometries; human reason is limited and faith takes on from there; God's super-universe is filled with life. He is not limited by human theology or rational argument or immoderate emotion. One cannot afford to let one's brain get in the way of his heart, or one's heart to get in the way of his brain. The spiritual is ever beyond our resolution, enough to cast only shadows, make whispers and hints at what we are seeing through the glass so darkly.

Counterpoint: Perhaps Human History Reveals-
"We the People" Cannot!

In this counter-argument, let me stand against the premise of this work. After all our known history, perhaps around 10,000 years, and as a species, perhaps 100,000 to one million years, what have we to show for our assumed skill of self-government? We have had centuries of religious, humanistic rationalism and 'all-in-between' philosophies, yet have never attained any utopia on our own.

The evidence, repeatedly is that we are in delusion to our ability of benevolent autonomy. Without God, we are just foolish and selfish, mutual opportunists enabling our illusions.

We have by our actions and words, in all of our own hypocrisies, erased our own nation. It is up to us, by the grace of God, to correct this tragedy. It is far more efficient to raise a *Third American Republic*, rather than try to clean a stubborn, rotted *tyranny*. But one asks, despite our worst characterizations, can *We* still govern ourselves with a more just and fair architecture for a democratic republic?

This present *Second American Republic* is fraught since its supposedly 'only' Civil War, the War Between the States; for some this 'War of Northern Aggression', has by its own history, failed to provide the full promise of life, liberty and the pursuit of happiness for all of its citizens. It has also masked the War Of 1812, as a 'second' American Revolution, from what was really its 'first' Civil War.

Let us again attempt to prove the present, unfulfilled theory to finally become a fact: that a people can govern themselves and all enjoy the fruits of such government, "of the people, by the people and for the people, so help us God".

Finally, a Serious Effort

Now with precedent, and prospectus as our latest foundation under God, let us with practicality endeavor this *Third American Republic*.

Because of our present level of personal interfacing in technology, we should each be able to directly represent ourselves domestically for the understanding of and the voting upon issues. If there is to be permitted lobbying, then all citizens are equally lobbied. In all cases the *People* remain governing fully. No need now for an Electoral College; any foreign ambassadors would be hired and in servitude to "We the People". If we choose to have a president, then that person will also be a servant of the *People*.

As a 'true republic' representing firstly "We the People", it would be expected of every corporation, commerce and individual citizen to be patriotic in all of their affairs. Patriotism is for the 'common good' of the *Third American Republic*; thus all servants of the republic are subject to the same laws and consequences. No citizen shall, because of position ever be immune from the law of the land.

In legal, political, commercial and military judgments, all is by vote of the majority through direct representation electronically. All interested parties will be allowed to present their views and then all of the citizens would decide by voting.

Committees of responsible citizens should self-assemble to reflect upon all issues pertinent to their shared interests and contributions. All citizens need to take their part in such representative assemblages. It has to be of importance enough to the citizenry to desire to govern, or all will eventually fail to an increasingly corrupt elite of selfish interests. The citizen is the only one on Earth with the ability to relinquish the right to its own 'self-government'. If the *People* governing themselves can strive to endure, then *"We the People"* really do need to govern ourselves.

Finally, America coming back to America!

Full Sovereignty for Native American Nations

As per the original intent of all treaties with the indigenous Native Americans and finally, in full respect of the sovereign state that each tribal entity is, then all lands are to be returned to their owners of origin.

Based on the Iroquois Confederacy, such as the Oneida Indian Nation, for example, all restored lands and independence are to be allowed without any hinderances. The Mohawks, Oneida, Onondaga, Cayuga and Seneca Nations are to be considered allies, as much as they and other Native American Nations are in agreement with the *Third American Republic*. Hopefully for all concerned, the past failures of the *First and Second American Republics'* repeated hypocrisies and breaking of treaties, should never happen again. Such sanctity for these nations should be their freedom from taxation, subjection under federal or state enforcements; for the Mohawk, Oneida, Onondaga and Seneca this is presently ongoing with harassment from state and federal authorities, and has been almost a constant of their history.

The unqualified 'empire-building' of the *First and Second American Republics* has stained these republics' reputations amongst the *Native American States*, as well as the 'silenced-citizens' of those republics. After living in anarchy with the extreme abuse and greed of democratic principles, the governments of the *First and Second Republics* over history have come to the point of losing the original confederation of the United States, beginning with its first 'civil' war, the War of 1812. For without patriotic or ethical restraint for the good of the *People*, these former republics have for most of their histories, been no more than governments of business tyranny.

When it was decided behind closed doors in 1867, that 'a corporation is a person', while never emphasizing or enforcing the same Constitutional right for the individual citizen equally, then the whole concept and premise of such a theory for the *People* to 'self- govern' was early lost. And thus far more, were the treaties and respect for the sovereignty of the Native American Nations abandoned.

To wit, now the upcoming economic advantages of these Native American Nations is far more for the better welfare of not only the Native Americans, but for the local and regional citizens nearby not of Native American descent.

Given enough time, the consequences of the earlier tyrannies that took over the *First and Second American Republic* have finally destroyed their own field of neo-feudalism. "We the People" with *The Third American Republic* can again govern ourselves. Now all citizens are governing, no longer being falsely represented.

Under God

To truly be a *Biblical Nation* under God, would follow the precedence set in God's Holy Word, the Bible- namely, Deuteronomy 17:14-20 and I Samuel 8: 1-22. Can we really have a Christian nation under God? Is this the most difficult of conditions being set forth for a people to claim they are a *Christian Nation*? If this is compromised, perhaps it is a great but not fully attainable ideal. It is likened to the proverbial mathematical limit, approached ever so closely, yet never there to arrive.

Citizen Reparations

It is considered that for reparations, as set by precedent of past history, "We the People" also deserve re-numeration for our historical sufferings. To really alleviate the stress of this present economic depression so denied by the present *Second American Republic*, then each citizen should receive a tax-free reimbursement for their part in stimulating the economy. Each *Third American Republic* citizen should receive, again tax-free $100,000. As there are no income taxes in the *Third American Republic*, and only limited property taxes of totally 10% of any and all properties per tax year, this should well propel from the ground up, an economic boon of savings, investments and purchases.

"We the People", after having tried to bring justice to all, have also need of justice finally, for ourselves. We, the people of the *Third American Republic* have ended our being robbed tyrannically by our false representatives, by realizing that we are really governing ourselves. A people can only endure so much as they allow themselves to endure. Our adversaries through history, have never denied their abuse of "We the People"; but that now has the reality to end by our own cooperative endeavors.

Inclusion, Expansion and Return to the British Commonwealth

A mature, responsible return to and association with the British Commonwealth would also be in order, maintaining as other Commonwealth members do, a national sovereignty while still serving all together for the greater common good, from citizen to state. For the *Third American Republic*, the greater advantage for both citizens and states would be the larger stage of all political, economic and defensive military for the common protection of all. Offensive military operations would have to be voted upon by the *Citizen Direct Representatives* of the *Third American Republic*, and be in consensus with the rest of the British Commonwealth.

Having traveled in my adult life several times within the British Commonwealth, I have witnessed, as other Americans over the years, a great social harmony, economic prosperity and military security, in the Bahamas, Barbados and Bermuda in particular. Racially, in commerce, defense and protection, they long ago achieved, without violent civil strife and tyrannical domination, what the United States up unto its present *Second American Republic* has found impossible to deliver.

Those of us Americans blessed to get outside the boundaries of the tyranny we find ourselves under, realize that perhaps the Revolution of 1776, the *civil* War of 1812, the War of Northern Aggression from 1861 to 1864 and the continual empire-building of un-patriotic corporate self-interests since the Grant Administration and all other offensive wars, have repeatedly been in vain of the promises of life, liberty and the pursuit of happiness of original intent since before our 'first' American Revolution.

We rebelled against our proper sovereign Great Britain, under King George, illegally; as it is written, rebellion is as witchcraft. We *were* colonies of a proper republic if we had continued to work within the system; a proper republic, not an anarchy of terrorists claiming to be provide 'democracy'.

Those who considered Great Britain to be the wiser and more ethical, were tarred and feathered and worse, by the false 'benevolence' of the anti-British 18th century terrorists, who would later attempt to re-write history to their quiet domination of the masses now subjected to them. They would follow the same decree as those of the French Revolution, only trading one 'tyranny' for another more real one. And the one tyranny they considered was following the laws of the land under their proper sovereign King George and Great Britain.

Great Britain proper, Canada and Australia seem less quiet perhaps for their sizes and their involvements with the present *Second American Republic's* global intrigues that have taken it far from its 'original intent' of its Articles of Confederation and Constitution.

A 'church' that claims to be based on the Bible and yet ignores that Holy Bible, is not really a church; then it is the same for an illegal, unethical 'republic' claiming only by corrupt practices, decrees and enforcement by tyranny, exposing its own hypocrisy of *not* following its original intent of the Articles of Confederation and the Constitution.

II Gettysburg Address

This 'second' Gettysburg Address is what would seem appropriate at our present dispensation of history, to be given on November 19, 2013.

"Seven score and ten years ago our fathers attempted to bring forth a new nation, conceived in liberty, and dedicated to the proposition that all men are created equal.

Now two *civil* wars, the first in 1812 and the second from 1861 to 1864, testing whether that nation, or any nation, so conceived and so dedicated can long endure. We are met on a great battlefield of the 'second' *civil* war, the War of States' Independence from unconstitutional federal unification and tyranny. We have come to reconsider those ideals not yet achieved, for those who gave their lives for their most cherished and differing causes, are herein buried. It is all together fitting and proper that we should do this.

But in a larger sense we cannot dedicate- we cannot consecrate- we cannot hallow- this ground. The brave men, now long dead, who struggled here, have consecrated it far above our poor power to add or detract. The world has little noted or long remembered what was said here before, and may not this day, but has somewhat forgotten what they did here. It is for us the living, rather, to be dedicated here to the still unfinished work which they who fought here have thus far, from each side, so nobly advanced. It is rather for us here to be dedicated to the great tasks- yet- before us- that for the honored dead we take increased devotion to those causes for which they each gave the last full measure of devotion; that we here highly resolve that all these dead shall not have died in vain from either side; that these two nations under God, would each have a new birth of freedoms- long promised yet long delayed; and that governments of the people, by the people, for the people, shall not perish from the earth." (© 2013 Robert B Cronkhite)

All of history and other nations have long witnessed the repeated failures of both the *First and Second American Republics*, two major civil wars and many minor conflicts on political, economic and territorial fronts.

In the *Third American Republic* there is no more 'public domain', stealing from a land's rightful owner, for the economic greed of a self-selected, more economically powerful few. We blatantly buy politicians who are for sale and shamefully ignore the established constitutional rights of individual citizens and states, under federal unifications of duress. To return to original intent of the founding fathers of the *First American Republic*, is to assert as measurable and ethically needed a *Third American Republic* "of the People, by the People, and for the People".

Resulting Logical Commentary

In a scientific venture of repeatable and verifiable evidence for the actual achievements and promises of the hopes and dreams of 'original intent' of the Articles of Confederation and the Constitution, both having been considered pieces of pretty paper increasingly by corrupt and illegally-based administrations, one only has to look at British Commonwealth. Again, without continual civil strife and turbulence, even violent tyrannical force, these promises, hopes and dreams have existed for almost two hundred years in the Bahamas, Barbados and Bermuda, specifically. If more Americans could travel, or even desire to travel, to these locations, then their present evaluations of their nation's reason for being, *raison d'etre*, would be obvious. No longer would they just assume what they are taught and told, while being so afraid of their present government as to not dare to ask or intelligently debate and build a really more secure, prosperous and ethical representative system.

Bantering in this work to the extremes of a 'direct-representative-republic', theorizing this *Third America* to even possibly needing to militarily constrain the present *Second American Republic*, considering that those Americans who are sincerely unhappy, frustrated and feeling so hindered to have to logically reassess their quality of life under the present *Second American Republic*, will have the fortitude, resolve, maturity and responsibility to really reacquire their rightful full citizenship in a *Third American Republic*.

The other educated and ethical decision, if a *Third American Republic* is not desired enough or resolvable enough, is to become British Citizens and receive the fuller advantages of the quality of life in the British Commonwealth.

The American Veteran has the most pertinent responsibility and deserves the full right to the quality of life he or she fought for, instead of being thrown away, ignored or worse, by the very nation for which they had assumed was worth the fight. Perhaps such full citizenship was always feared by the 'Originators'. Why else since the Electoral College to the present blatant, hypocritical domination and restraint of citizens' full possibilities and promises of *republic freedom* has perpetuated in favor of prostituted career politicians who profit from this unpatriotic, corporate, tyrannical, self-interested anarchy.

Since the piracies of supposed 'Reconstruction' from the Grant Administration through to the present day, America as 'originally' intentioned has been dead and gone. Then without allowing question or debate by a proper full *constitutional citizenry*, the empire- builders took over from within. Even after the Revolution and through the *War of Northern Aggression* of the early United States, private and selfish interests slowly bought their way to power as a fifth economic column of invasion from within. It was intended to be a republic for all, patriotism for all, corporate and business included. The illegal buying from within only exposed the failure of a people to be able to govern themselves, unless they can buy their power. The evolving, tyrannical, empire-building government slowly became the antithesis of its own foundation.

Now it has so corrupted itself from within, its prisoner citizens are finally realizing that they have to take and maintain their rightful duty of self-government or accept the fact that they are really unable. If they cannot, then the best, based on the evidence of history, is to return to the logical, proper and rightful authority of the British Commonwealth. Political stubbornness is no balm for an allowed and excused 'tyranny'.

And another point: since the Reconstruction Period the

real reason for Eminent Domain has been for the benefit of those unpatriotic corporations that bought the *Second American Republic's* government; we have already been under, the *'American- Soviet Socialist Republic'*. Trying to beat the Russian Communist system, only has made us so like them that the subtle difference is left to geography. We need to return to the proper 'origins of intent' of the Articles of Confederation and the Constitution.

Some of the other countries under the British Commonwealth like the Bahamas, Belize and Bermuda and even third world countries like Costa Rica do not have career politicians or 'eminent domain'. The *Second American Republic* by corruption has watered down the great documents' values, such as the Declaration of Independence, the Articles of Confederation and the United States Constitution! These afore-mentioned nations also filter much more for the common good and the perpetuity of their nations' immigration.

Liberalism has only brought us another tyranny by these hours and days in our 21st Century. For so many- wanting of free thought, yet without hypocrisy or the lack of needed ethics, and without any more hidden agendas for tyrannical power to again quietly undermine the greater good- there still awaits a better way of government. It will take patience and action, forethought and dedication, and the collaboration of like-minded, decent individuals.

As recently alluded to, the British Commonwealth has over the last two hundred plus years grown, matured and prospered. It has become a powerfully-maintained presence in the world and very important to not only the maintenance of peace and security in the world, but civilization itself.

Watching, at this writing still within the waning days of the *Second American Republic*, how 'Britannia', as I like to call *The Commonwealth*, is itself the emergence, quietly over time, of a *Second British Empire*. Perhaps the United States has been slowly coming back home to the motherland, from which it had only for a time chose to run away.

Britannia is still ruling and the sun still does not set upon her vast endeavor. Perhaps the *Third American Republic* would do better just to cooperate, collaborate and return to its more proper place as of original intent, to its parental intended-design; and then be able to more honestly and responsibly be a government "of the People, by the People and for the People".

This resurgent *Second British Empire*, this prolifically prosperous and mature British Commonwealth, 'Britannia', is what is to become dominant. It is a cradle of advancing civilization without need of wars to foster economic growth, without need for internal civil strife and insurrections to indicate failures of its inherent design. This 'Britannia' may be what the almost, incessant, turbulent history of the 'United' States could have been; promising so much, yet requiring either military force or abandonment of its 'origins of intent', its Constitution, and its Articles of Confederation; or both, to strong arm even its own citizens to submission.

We know it by its fruits, as those who under its domestic tyranny endure. One knows one is not to ask the wrong questions, really take seriously the tenets of the constitutional, protected promises, not to buck against, even legally, the regime really in power that masks as 'benefactor'. Serve in its armed forces, not allowing oneself to be brainwashed into a fearful compliant, entertained and well-fed state of following without discernment of orders, and one realizes something is wrong. We realize there is more to life, liberty and the pursuit of happiness than just consuming oneself in submission to idolatry, that seduction that has been made manifest in this society. One realizes that "We the People", is not to be pursued. The citizen's true value of being 'an American' is so well questioned by the minority who can desire and afford to leave its dominion for other lands for a time, especially to the British Commonwealth.

Try to really make a difference outside of established, *authorized* institutions, whether scientific, literary or other academic areas, and one is limited by the 'regime' truly in power. Even the voting is so controlled that fair elections are not allowed by any outside third parties. Today, one must "take it or leave it", realizing enough educated and intelligent frustration to make improvements, or just submit and be allowed to 'enjoy' without any unconstitutional interference.

There never has been a perfect human government, without God. But there are degrees of quality within governments throughout history and presently. And for the United States in 2013 AD, it is of the utmost embarrassment to be unable to maturely and honestly handle the PFC Bryan Manning and Mr. Edward Snowden affaires. Here, the *Second American Republic* has finally gone so far as a 'rogue' government to destroy the relevance of value of its *Documents of Origin*- the Constitution, the Articles of Confederation and the Declaration of Independence, and more.

Why 'rogue'?   Because the government has felt, that during and since the end of the *War of the Rebellion, War Between the States,* or *War of Northern Aggression,* that it had to usurp the Constitution in order to enforce 'union'. Even President Lincoln had to set aside Constitutional principle with the denial of *habeaus corpus* for individuals and the shutting down of disagreeing newspapers!

Though President Lincoln was a wonderful president in many ways, he still set quite the precedent of limiting the full expression of the Constitution during the Civil War, in contrast with the *First Repbulic's* original intent for the supposedly 'democratic' republic

With the arrival of 2013 AD, the Manning and Snowden situations (that have given us two modern-day 'Nathan Hales') and Julian Assange ('Thomas Jefferson'), we also have Unmanned Aerial Vehicles (UAVs), half of which are to be used against *American civilians*, in 'non-combat' situations, on our own *domestic soil*! Again, without verifiable evidence and using Napoleanic Law, where one is guilty until proven innocent, the United States' *rogue*, unconstitutional government has become tyrannical and out of control. Even with secret and closed 'judicial' proceedings, just plain witch-hunts are only perpetuated.

To its own shame, the participants of this present 'rogue' state allow no consequence to their own and have let the world now know how dangerous and despicable they really are; forcing all under them to dare not question the constitutionality of their procedures. Enough 'bread and circus' have for many Americans allowed them to not take responsibility for their present state of government. After enough generations have passed, even such a wonderful gift of God has finally rotted so within that it has left a tragic, hypocritical joke upon the world. Russia has played this to excellent geo-political poker and is enabling the United States finally to reassess its worth in the world mirror. Supposedly, the government of the United States *won* the Cold War, yet it has lost its respect and exposed its facades.

Now is the time for "We the People" to either purge this *second* American 'republic' and replace it with a true, Constitutional *Third American Republic*, or admit defeat and failure, then to return to the original intent of the British Commonwealth as a participating state.

It is with fascination that it looms so significantly, that we humans may not really be able to govern ourselves, with our slight bias of self-determination to just try to.

"Dare we scientifically/mathematically quantify the reality of a people to self-govern?"

Hoping, even if based on the fifty-fifty odds of probability favoring our really being able to make such desire work. Now in such thinking, as odds of a flipping penny, we may now speculate our possibilities herein. That, with an almost infinitesimally thin penny to better approach the limit of 'fifty-fifty', we have some mechanism to further our dreams of such social and political contemplation.

Consider that the thicker the penny, the less and less it will approach the 'fifty-fifty' limit and for the penny to be, it has to have an edge. The thinner the penny, then nearer to 50/50 as per games of so called 'chance', we would more practically consider, around 47/47, with the six remaining as some "out of our ability to control" variance.

Now that we have become mathematically mechanistic to the approach of our ideal, we should look at history. The past's solid course reveals the future's tendency, while many of the details remain hidden until they become the present. In time, with proper detective methods, more details can be articulated from what we at such a present time know.

This probability of 47/47 and adding the bias of our lack of objectivities in our decisions so very often, now appears more reasonable. Even the outright, seemingly Shakespearian-madness in our methods of making a stuttered progress, we so often take two steps forward and then one back; so perhaps this may help us indicate from our variance of six, we may over time add a bias of three on our progressive side and subtract three from the other regressive side. So now with 53/44 as the historical progress, and our possibly being too optimistic yet, perhaps we are able, by such slim margins, to govern ourselves.

Such a slim margin demands extraordinary qualities in a people actually meeting the requirements to self-govern. Not even the whole population has to meet the same level of quality. Some perhaps looking at a statistical Bell Curve could say that with 80% doing their best with mediocre quality, and 10% with exceptional quality, and allowing for another 10% being a social and political burden of the governing, we now seem to better see how 53/44 is more realistic of a people to self-govern.

Taking a sampling of our experiences and observations of life, each of us in comparing our republic's past with its present should be able to sense how our qualities and population match the practical demands afore-mentioned. Are we an ethical and self-motivated people? Do we desire education not only in the academic, but the practical? Do we have what it takes? These are important questions for every citizen to assess in themselves and those around them.

With technology, we are grappling the proverbial 'two-edged sword'; some of us are progressing, some of us are regressing, some of us are somewhere along that middle curve of the statistical Bell type graph. Now place in context how we really are; how much bias could we estimate to add or subtract from our 53/44 favoring? Quantifying in this way our present social and political quality helps us to actually evaluate, especially after more than two hundred years, our ability to truly self-govern.

If I were permitted to sell you stock with such a history, with a now somewhat measurability of the quality of people, would you buy this stock with your life savings? Making it personal this way, the Bell Curve helps us all realize that to achieve true self-government may require a modification of our percentages.

If we find that we really *do* have a spoiled, selfish, unethical society at all levels, and far more than we care to admit, then perhaps after over two hundred years of our historical statistics, truer progression may be found by our returning to some type of aristocracy with such a higher needed demand, and more than 10%. If we also are seeing a smaller than 80% of middle level achievers, perhaps we are more so seeing that we have actually progressed to a return to the society against whom we had a revolution. In time people tend to take the path of least resistance and return to a place where they are parented socially and politically.

After over two hundred years, with available education, more advanced technology, more selfish leisure, would we not observe a richer, more fulfilled and progressed social and political order?

If I may, I should like to propose that after all the numbers and history are considered, that after more than two hundred years we so well "chat ourselves up", but in reality we are just a modern, sophisticated, feudalistic society, as all human societies are from the stone age to this corporate age.

It is said that there is an '80/20 rule', and that human society tends to have a reoccurring ratio of the ruled to the ruler; more people work for someone than run a business administrating others; more people are governed than govern. This very old rule has been another quantifier of our considerations. Why, just look at our modern society from Las Vegas to Detroit and Pittsburgh to New York and Washington, DC.

Go into a casino, and theirs is the fruit of our two hundred years of history.

We are making it an expression of what we believe we can do; what possibility to really obtain. Are we capable and willing enough to really govern ourselves? For if we really cannot, we actually will not; then we never did deserve the brief blessing God had given us to be a sincere "We the People". It shall only in time return to tyranny rule, as we again only prefer to satisfy our baser addictive comforts, conveniences and pleasures.

In other words, it takes a very remarkable *People* to govern themselves and have progress. For all of our intentions, declarations and self-glorifications we statistically have returned, in our 'bread and circus', to over time willfully submit ourselves under another tyranny. We have had to have revolution, two 'civil' wars and many upon many turbulent episodes; and after getting to the Moon, we surrendered to comfort, convenience and its tyrannical benefactors.

A corporations is legally a person, while conveniently a person is not legally a corporation. The corporate feudal technological state is what we have chosen to become. Capitalism supposedly denounces socialism for the individual, while encouraging corporate socialism for its benefactors, its corporate owners. We love to be taken care of, have entertainment and feed ourselves to lack of health, while those really in power have grown more powerful.

Is there any question of a corporation's patriotism? Corporate states are what has survived and thrived, despite our supposed intentions and declarations. Are the corporations entirely wrong? No, for we love being ruled, as long as our rulers give us a gilded cage.

Again, after reflecting on our often-cited ideals and lofty commendations, what have we all really witnessed of this society and its real possibility of governing itself? So, I ask again, would you buy this stock with your life savings?

Another question is how we shall represent ourselves? 'Representative' government has only brought us elite or career politicians. We vote for them, but since the Constitution is not enforced, they have wound up our feudal masters. These career politicians represent only those who bribe them through lobbyists. We pay for their pensions and their various insurance needs, and they receive Social Security benefits; they have allowed themselves to be immune from the consequence of law, perhaps including tax-evasion and never contributing to Social Security.

So what is the solution? With our personal computers, *Direct Representation* is the only alternative!

If the *Republic's* legal citizens do not exercise their responsibilities, then all this is in vain. A 'corporation is a person', but it does not mean that a person is a corporation. If corporate socialism is set by precedent for corporations, then logically all persons should as well reap the same subsidizing.

So far, Russian has been winning the Cold War, which never really ended, despite buying many of our representative political prostitutes; and Great Britain has finally won the *American Revolution*. Many of us have already for years been returning to the British Commonwealth for example, Australia, Canada, Ireland, and the Bahamas, Barbados, Bermuda and other areas of *The Commonwealth*.

Interestingly consider this concept, as per the *Rights of the States*: Why do the States have to continue assuming the '*ir*-responsibilities' of an un-constitutional, coerced union's federal 'government'? The states have no constitutional liability to assume any debts, not constitutionally-based, of the federal government. In other words, the states if standing on their Constitutional base, do **not** have to assume any of the federally derived debts. Washington's irresponsibility are then **null** and **void**.

Thusly, the delusions of a federal debt are baseless on the states' level. If it means secession and '*re-Confederation*' as originally intended, then so be it. Again, all such reinterpretations, even ignoring willfully and unconstitutionally our Articles of Confederation, the Declaration of Independence and the Constitution, are of a new illegal basis.

Looking at the Province of Quebec, Canada is a bold illustration of a region's own local exercise of sovereignty compared to its federal government. Those who chose to live in Quebec, should live as **Les Quebecois** live.

So if need be, because of resistance from the **Second American Republic's** being bought with such a price to allow itself over a century to be tyrannical, should our present coerced union be dissolved? What has it accomplished that its need for debt ceilings and default are required?

Rather, the **Third American Republic,** being free of all prior debts of the **Second American Republic**, without income taxes and without oppressive, self-serving, political interests, can be a very commercially vibrant mechanism.

Some will not join us; but for those of us willing to pursue this avenue to redeem the America we were promised by our forefathers, we shall reap what we have been allowed to be sown.

It is written, "If my people, who are called by My Name, shall humble themselves, and pray, and seek My Face, and turn from their wicked ways; then I will hear from heaven, and will forgive their sin, and will heal their land." (II Chronicles 7:14)

It is up to **each** of us citizens, not just **some** of us. May we instead of suffering in fear and silence under a tyranny for over 140 years, finally be the active "We the People" we were supposed to be. Otherwise, to whine and fret, and not practice our God-given responsibilities, leave us without excuse or complaint.

It was Captain Eddie Rickenbacker who said, "Courage is doing what you're afraid to do. There can be no courage unless you're scared." Also someone else said "that for victory, there are a thousand fathers, but defeat is left an orphan ".

Now it is up to **you**; may God's will be done.

This Union is Now Dissolved

"This Union is now dissolved"- not to be taken lightly, but with much somber reflection.

No nation is perfect, and neither will that nation be that replaces the United States in its present design and function as 'second' of republics that may sequentially follow in due course. The original *First Republic,* based on the Constitution was thus ruined by the unconstitutionally, unethically-based railroad and other large businesses whose only interests were themselves. It was the *Second Republic's* use of 'eminent domain' that allowed unpatriotic profiteers to without legal consequence, just steal and lie their way in taking from the *People,* their hardwired properties and other assets.

We shall not desire the problem that occurred during the French Revolution of the 18th century, when despite the overthrow of the aristocrats and nobility, the *People* had traded one tyranny for another. Despite all their *liberte, egalite,* and *fraternite,* they more often than not found their liberation before a guillotine. We do not want another Robespierre in our midst; we are not looking for any excuse for a counter-revolution, as had occurred. What is needed is a peaceable, fair and open restructuring in the least amount of time; thus to avoid complicating non-essential tangents that might interfere with our *Third American Republic* getting settled and working, so that all of the citizens may enjoy life, liberty and the pursuit of happiness.

A union dissolved does not mean there is no organization of law, order and justice, and that anarchy reigns. No, what is required is a better confederation of cooperation, without coercion. Again, the weak and suffering are not at the mercy of the unethically strong. We are not trading one tyranny for another. The betterment of our *People* is for what we strive. If in time, we will not or cannot attain that which would be for our better intentions, then we do not deserve that which is better.

Why a 'confederation' and not a 'federation' of States is a result of the prior *Second American Republic's* history. We cannot allow again usurping of power to a stronger selfish few, whether economic, military or political. Otherwise, one revolution will breed the contempt over time for another; such has been human history for ages. The hope is that, despite the elements of corruption and illegality always present in any society, a *nation* can stay above in its ethics and maturity to seek and foster the betterment of its *citizens*.

This "union now dissolved" requires swiftly a social-political order up to the task; in place, ready and willing to engage the required establishments, institutions and progress that it has so suddenly replaced. That is the reason for such to have a day, an hour and a place from which it is prepared to begin its duties for the "*We the People*".

As a template, let us establish as the place and time, Oklahoman City, OK (as the capital and seat of the new *confederation*), 1200 noon Eastern Daylight Time on the fourth day of July 2014, (or 2015 or 2016). At that place and at that time, Washington, D.C. is null and void of all power, real or imagined on their part. At that place and time, it does not matter to "We the People" what our perspectives are, they are null and void. An illegal conglomeration without consent of the *People*, and if surrounded by now *Third American*-sympathetic military forces, then they which have built Guantanamo Bay for their form of 'justice' shall there be detained and tried for treason. For is not treason a judgment upon those not adhering legally to the Constitution in its 'original intent', with malice and subversion to the original *First Republic*? It is sad that we need a *Third American Republic* so that we can return to the legality of rule, since the Civil War of 1861 to 1864 was ignored by 'unionization'.

"What goes around, comes around", as it should be for those evading by illegal decree their responsibilities and consequences; there in, they shall not be immune from those laws based upon the original intent of "We the People".

Having established a place and time for the new republic, it is for the best interest of the *People* to before then to have in place some type of decisive, legal, constitutionally-based government, ready to convene and pursue an effective, considerate and cooperative administration.

This *Third Americian Republic*, finally our own, beginning with the majority to the minority will all be equally represented. The *Fifth Estate* is made up of all of the citizens, "We the People" firstly governing and secondly, being governed; our use of the Internet and other means based upon the Constitution, will be of vital importance in our representation.

The *Fourth Estate* will include an objective public-sponsored media and the republic media; accurate and timely information is essential for *The People* who will ultimately approve all of the *Third American Republic's* functions.

The *Third Estate* of 'commoners', will include those citizens who cannot participate or may choose not to fully participate for personal issues or reasons, but are essntial in securing the progress and advancement of their nation.

The *Second Estate* is the 'nobility', or better in these times those who may have noble and honorable qualities in high positions of business and commerce for our mutual prosperity. They are the 'gifted ones', not self-serving, of whom we hold in high regard due to their benefits to society as a whole; but who we now hold accountable lest they become dangerous un-constitutional demagogues of tyranny, usurping self-power all over again in the decades to follow.

The *First Estate* will consist of those of our *Christian Zionist Faith* who will guide us with the Biblical principles to which we adhere; again precedent has been set in the efforts of the basis of support for a so-called Palestinian State.

Preparatory to the emergence in function of this 'breath of social-political fresh air', this *Third American Republic*, is the months of organizing and planning required, for what some would claim to be a *Post-American* world; but rather one that has been already for over 160 years without a legally based *American Republic*. Since the so called 'Civil War', really *The War Between the States* or *The War of Northern Aggression*, which the 'union', by military coercion, has been a facade of tyranny that has too long tried to fool the *People* and the world.

This 'union' has for so long oppressed honest opinion to the point that too many generations have been 're-educated' to accept this present theatre as the real *intentioned* government. The *People* have slowly come to realize this because of the recent, courageous revelations by Assange, Manning, Snowdon and other citizens finally fed up with the delusions of those in power, only for themselves, buying the representatives of this *Second Republic*. It is up to you, and all of us 'Americans' to dare to make the difference required .... or to just surrender and never have a basis upon which to complain.

Again, and I have to reiterate that we *must* have the courage and persistence to bring back this country to ourselves. It has been too long, for so many to be intoxicated by 'bread and circus' and the vaporish ownership allowed; as long as those in tyrannical power deem to take and steal what the *People* have worked and strived for, they will continue to claim that 'eminent domain' is their right.

Thinking scientifically and objectively, the *Post-American* world occurred in 1861 when military intervention was brought in to suppress the will of those Americans who chose, by constitution right to secede from the imperfect union, legally but that the Constitution had no restrictions for such actions. Now is obtainable a land where, with constant, constitutional vigilance a nation "of the People, by the People, for the People shall not perish from the earth".

It is written, "Righteousness exalteth a nation: but sin is a reproach to any people."(Proverbs 14:34). And it is so that history bears this out over and over, from the midst of ancient civilizations- ancient Sumer, Egypt, Greece and Rome- unto our historical modern times; with special emphasis for our present situation. From the French Revolution of the 18th century to today in our 21st century with technology, corporate states and swift transfer of information, the relevance is astounding of how those not caring to study history, are blatantly repeating it.

With 'indirect representation' many problems have arisen, but now with the internet, *direct* representation by "We the People" is possible. No longer will the citizen be separate, out of the direct action and reaction of consideration and understanding; but a living part of the very process for which the *People* is held accountable. Now the 'Proletariat' within the *Fifth Estate* is finally governing and being governed by one's own peers, the citizenry.

Does this all seem so idealistic? Are the theories of self-government really able to survive ground truth? Does the present *Second American Republic* fear such a revelation, based on its own promulgations of such promises for decades? Why stoke such dreams from the founding of the *First American Republic*? ... yet which by 1861, had to enforce its survival by such tyranny and coercion, that it had no longer survived intact but had been replaced by illusion and manipulation.

Previously I had tried to play a counter-point in that human self-government is not possible. To even speak and publish such commentaries as this book, is fearful to many. If that is the case, then does not this reaction expose the fruit of such oppressive action? Why promote such illusion, and then punish those who act upon their believing it?

It is but a matter of time that things are revealed, to an individual and to a People. Truth will come in its time: "Time's glory is to calm contending kings, expose falsehood and bring truth to light"; "Friends, Romans, countrymen, lend me your ears; I come to bury Caesar not to praise him"; "*Sic sempre tyrannis* thus, always to tyrants". Even Mr. Shakespeare would concur for he had so succinctly portrayed humanity from the results of its own follies. By our so often fruitions are we so known; thus our histories.

Can I dare to enjoy the possibilities of human self-government that will not denigrate into an anarchy to have to be again put down? Why proclaim such, only to offer a gilded cage to allow for the perpetration of a few, while the delusional toils of many? Why not a government really of, by and for the *People*?

If on this courageous and noble course we all choose to journey, and each of us to take our better part for the grander cause, then we shall really obtain what we all so many times have desired. What a noble hero of ethics we can try to attain; and then be able to progress forward for a better land in which to live and work and rest and dream.

But for human frailty, the failure of motives once noble, as is the major case of history, shall succumb to our demise. A candle is a delicate thing to enjoy and yet if too strong a breeze, so easily blown out. This we should not allow. May I dare say, we *must* not allow? Do we have the social and political fortitude to blaze bravely against an ill wind? Perhaps we are a too delicate, lovely, warm, comforting flame. Perhaps, I ponder too much that which is most likely to be expected, too greatly … my own great expectations.

What then are our alternatives? … saying nothing and

surrendering to a soft, sometimes hard tyranny; only enjoying what we are allowed to indulge in per food and entertainment; keeping our rights of an opinion to ourselves, so that we constantly murmur, only away from the 'thought and talk' police. Do we live in fear and dread of our neighbors, those in commercial institutions as per banks and even the receptionists pools of the medical 'professionals'; to be afraid of those who love to play or watch dogs? But we fear that 'they' secretly *report* anyone toward whom they socially and politically harbor resentment or jealously in their work with the common public (in their pathological 'guarding' for the oppressive, social, political order). Remember, 'they' want to get paid and keep their jobs for the meager power and profit, while prostituting their public service position and worse denying the Constitution for their own advantages. 'They' also are the ones who claim to be *patriotic*, while rotting the same from within. Of these socio-politcal-paths, we must be wary.

Rather it is a brave thing far more to uphold the ethics of the rights given by God and the Constitution unto all its citizens, despite those oft-overlooked domestic and foreign saboteurs of what our *American Republic* was 'originally' meant to be. This has not been new, but has been perpetuated since the *Founding* because of those who by no matter what, profit of self-gain and power. All along while they have held up to the public eye their supposed 'terrorists', and in prior times 'communists, spies and anarchists', while far more profoundly aiding and abetting that same of their own within!

Let us, each of us, dare to really live and pursue quietly and actively the *Founders Original Intentions* for our neighbor and for ourselves. Let us have the courage and fortitude to each of us do our part for the betterment of the all of our *Third American Republic*.

There have been and now also are the times that "We the

People" need to *ourselves* take the reins of power in their proper manner; to govern ourselves as *We, Ourselves* are governed. This is achievable if we really desire to put into practice a sincere and ambitious 'citizenship'. There will always be the danger that some 'Robespierres' will surface and attempt to consolidate power- economic, political or social- unto themselves. Yet, let all be allowed to make profit, without income tax, to truly receive what one has earned. Thus allowing profit at any amount to be attained by anyone, as long as it is not used as an economic weapon upon the *Original Intentions* of our legal proper form of republic. Such economic warfare from within or without is as dangerous as such the same physical weapons of war.

The only common tax at appropriately no more than 10% and whatever is proper upon import/export duties is far more than enough, despite despotic-intentioned claims. The subtle and surface public, national 'welfare' propaganda, when more wisely considered is only the most polished of thieves taking of your wallet, while helping you look for it.

If any of us choose to become slovenly in our sober pursuit of a sincere *Third American Republic,* then as time goes by and others also fall to that side, perhaps generations, we may again lose what was 'originally intended', and we will again have no one to blame but ourselves.

For those of us who believe in God's grace, we also recognize as the same our responsibilities of decision and intent. For the rest of us, Shakespeare, as usual said it so well, "Men at some times are masters of their fates: The fault, dear Brutus is not in our stars, but in ourselves, that we are underlings". So let me considerately and wisely add, "Beware the ides of March".

In the end, after the most brave and well-prepared of endeavors we may just have to face a *Post-American* world. This ground truth of history has to come, so essential is it in the objective science of things and their mechanism in order to reveal such a reality. All this, despite the most intense of theory and repeatedly verifying facts, which separates the wise, humble, experienced persons from the presumptuous, arrogant, naive person. It is to be the final summation of around three hundred years plus of humanity's experiment of the so far 'theory of self-government'. Throughout history wars, suffering and inequality have seemed to surface as the fruits of such the 'noblest', human, rationalist's intentions for the 'betterment of the common good'. A fruit so close, yet unattainable.

If the education of true history with scientific objectivity can be an indicator, we are on an uphill climb, and we have bitten off more than we can chew. For this all would have been attained in our cumulative past, thus with the supporting anthropological and archaeological evidence.

Will we instead only demonstrate in the history to come, the futility of human self-government? How do we ameliorate the past coercion to 'union', to 'united' which has since the revolution had so much fruition in more civil, economic, political and social strife. Such turmoil requires strongly-enforced order, at such times internal civil or even military violent suppression. Thus resulting in over history small complements of "life, liberty and the pursuit of happiness", so oft promised. It is written in the Scriptures, as "a cloud that promises rain, but passes over delivering (little or) none"; sadly our history has so surmised.

It is possible for all the grand ideals of *Original Intent* to bloom and proliferate for all and not just the few. Perhaps a better cooperative of commerce and industry, for each of us to keep what we earn and thus in such fair capitalism, without any elitist, corporate, political socialism, might allow all of us a mighty commerce to make; finally, a capitalism unknown to any hinderance by a seductive thieving few. Cooperation with gain and not by tyranny, overt or subtle, "of the People, by the People, for the People", that this time "shall not perish from the earth".

Here on, which after much forethought, reflection and the limited permissibility remaining at these hours for the sharing of intelligently procured ideas, this is all very much up to each and every one of us, and all very, very much up to *you.*

"The world is grown so bad, that wrens make prey where
eagles dare not perch",
Richard III (Act I, Scene III), William Shakespeare
-Fin-